W9-AQH-113

Marvelous Measurement

Lisa Arias

rourkeeducationalmedia.com

Scan for Related Titles
and Teacher Resources

Before & After Reading Activities

Level: **P** Word Count: **623 Words**

100th word: ***the* page 10**

Before Reading:

Building Academic Vocabulary and Background Knowledge

Before reading a book, it is important to tap into what your child or students already know about the topic. This will help them develop their vocabulary, increase their reading comprehension, and make connections across the curriculum.

1. *Look at the cover of the book. What will this book be about?*
2. *What do you already know about the topic?*
3. *Let's study the Table of Contents. What will you learn about in the book's chapters?*
4. *What would you like to learn about this topic? Do you think you might learn about it from this book? Why or why not?*
5. *Use a reading journal to write about your knowledge of this topic. Record what you already know about the topic and what you hope to learn about the topic.*
6. *Read the book.*
7. *In your reading journal, record what you learned about the topic and your response to the book.*
8. *After reading the book complete the activities below.*

Content Area Vocabulary

Read the list. What do these words mean?

capacity
conversion
customary units
exclusively
gram
length
liter
mass
measurement
meter
metric system
precisely
unit
weight

After Reading:

Comprehension and Extension Activity

After reading the book, work on the following questions with your child or students in order to check their level of reading comprehension and content mastery.

1. *Explain how a fluid is measured. (Summarize)*
2. *Why do some countries use the metric system while others use the customary system? (Asking questions)*
3. *What is the difference between customary and metric systems? (Summarize)*
4. *Why is it important to have different units for measuring how long something is and how heavy something is? (Asking questions)*
5. *When should you use a ruler? When should you use a yardstick? (Infer)*

Extension Activity

Let's see how you measure up! How would you measure how tall you are: a ruler or yardstick? Which unit would you use to state your weight: ounce, pound, or ton? Using a piece of paper create a table with one side being your height and the other your weight. Write a guess for each. Write which units you would use for each and what tools you will use to obtain your measurements. Measure and weigh yourself. Were you close to your guess? What tools worked best?

Table of Contents

Measurement 4
Measurement Systems 6
Customary Units 10
Customary Weight 18
Customary Capacity 20
Metric Units 24
Glossary 30
Index 31
Websites to Visit 31
About the Author 32

Measurement

How big, how tall?
How heavy, how small?

Measurement allows us to agree
on the exact **length**, **weight**, and **capacity**
things should be.

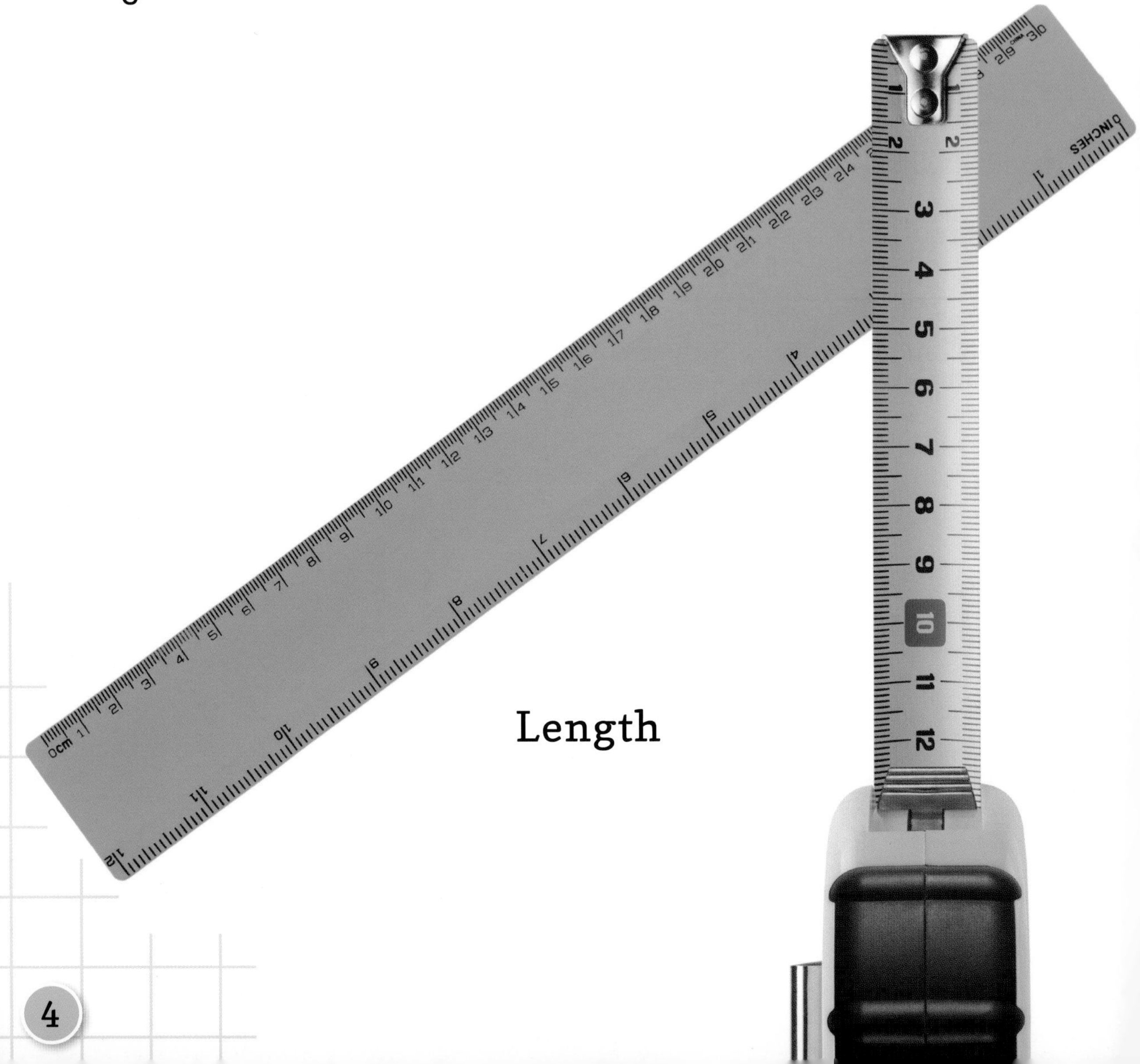

Length

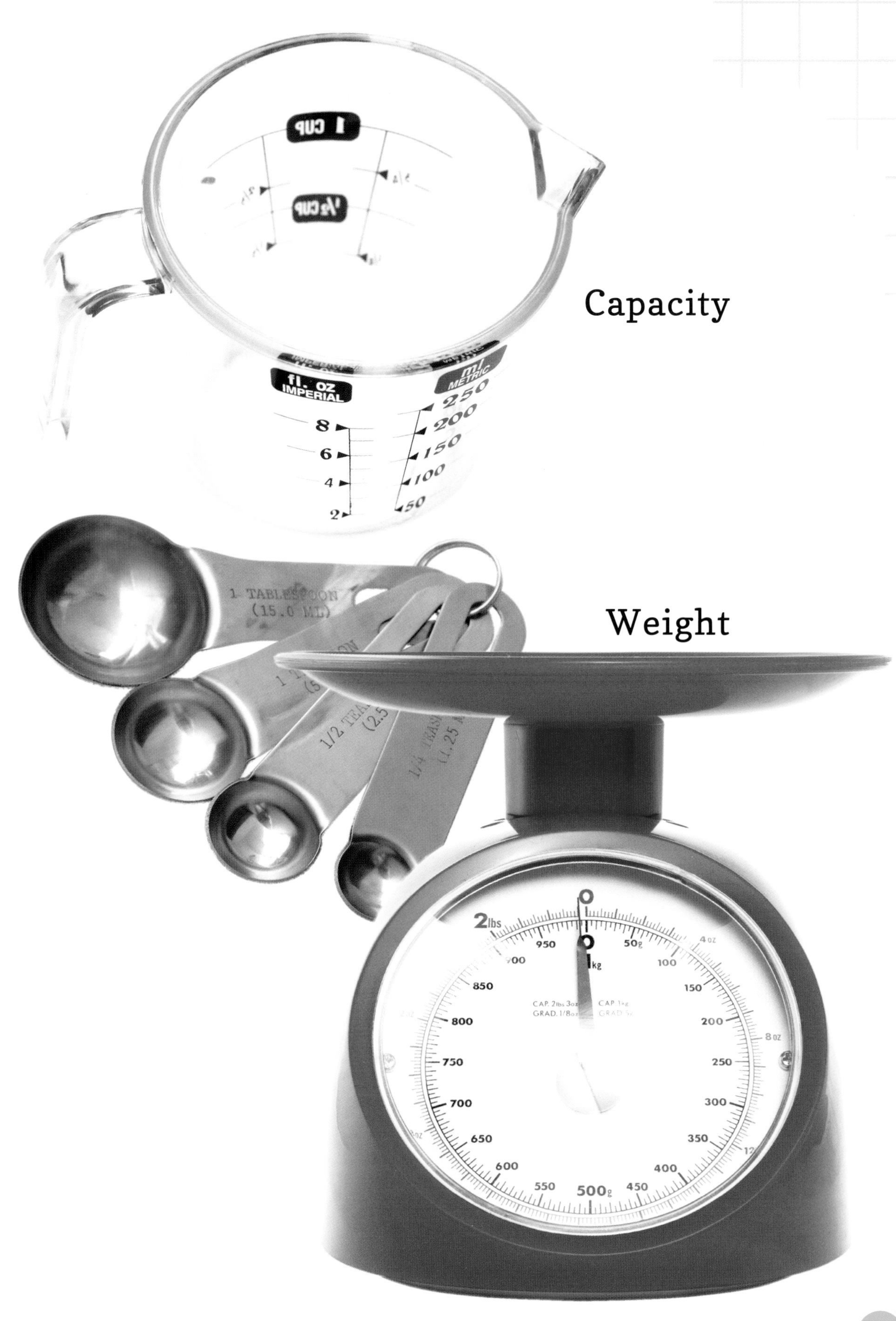
Capacity
Weight
1 CUP
1/2 CUP
fl. oz
IMPERIAL
ml
METRIC
8
6
4
2
250
200
150
100
50
1 TABLESPOON
(15.0 ML)
2lbs
0
950
50g
900
100
850
150
800
200
750
250
700
300
650
350
600
400
550
500g
450
CAP. 2lbs 3oz
GRAD. 1/8oz
CAP. 1kg
8oz

Measurement Systems

The world has yet to agree on which **unit** of measurement to use **exclusively**.

The **metric system** by far is most popular.

The U.S. has it best, measuring with **customary units** as well as metric, unlike most of the rest.

Measurement Systems Used by Country

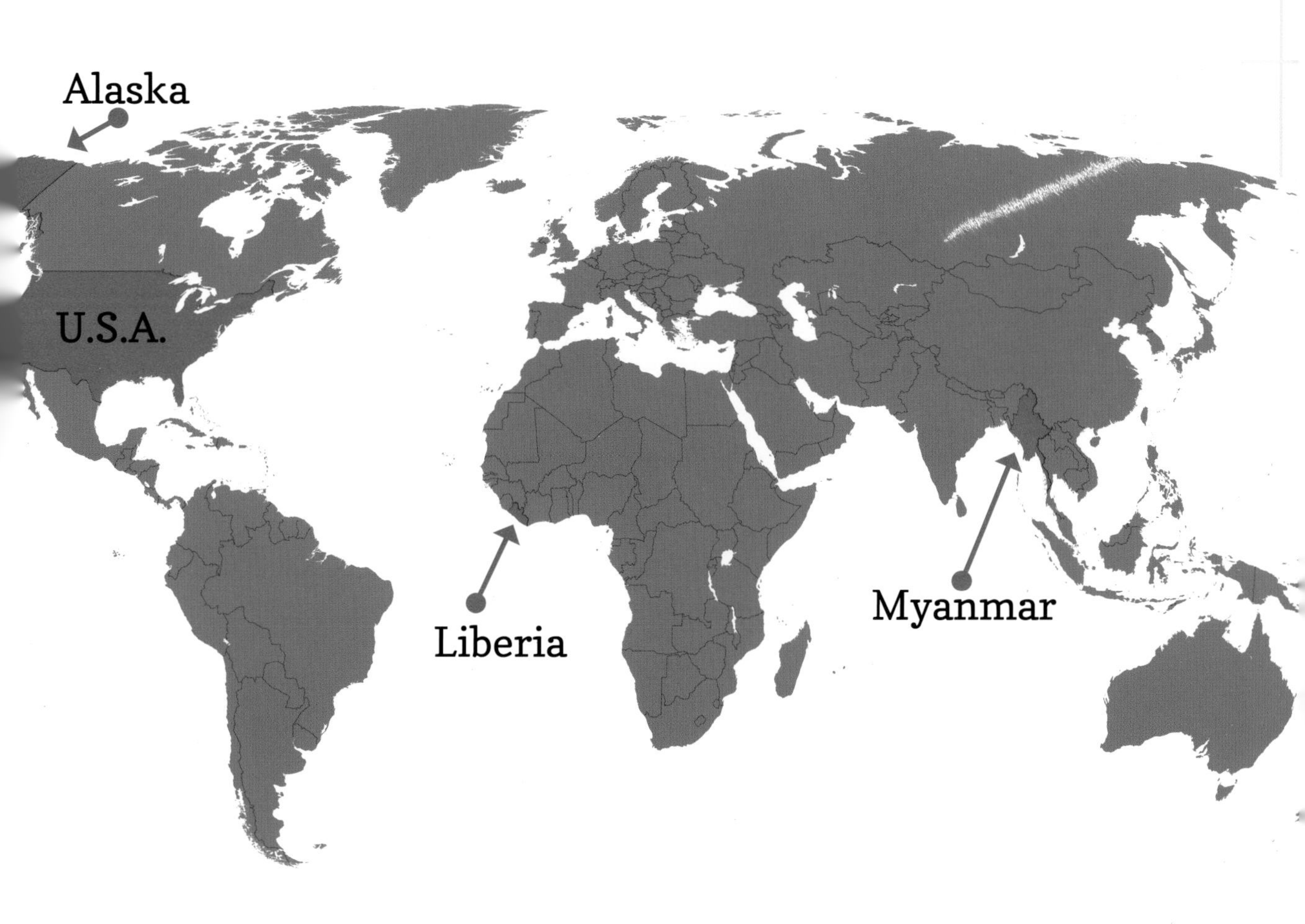

Countries using the metric system

Countries using customary units and metric system

Things are measured in units no matter what system is used.

Look at each chart to tell the units apart.

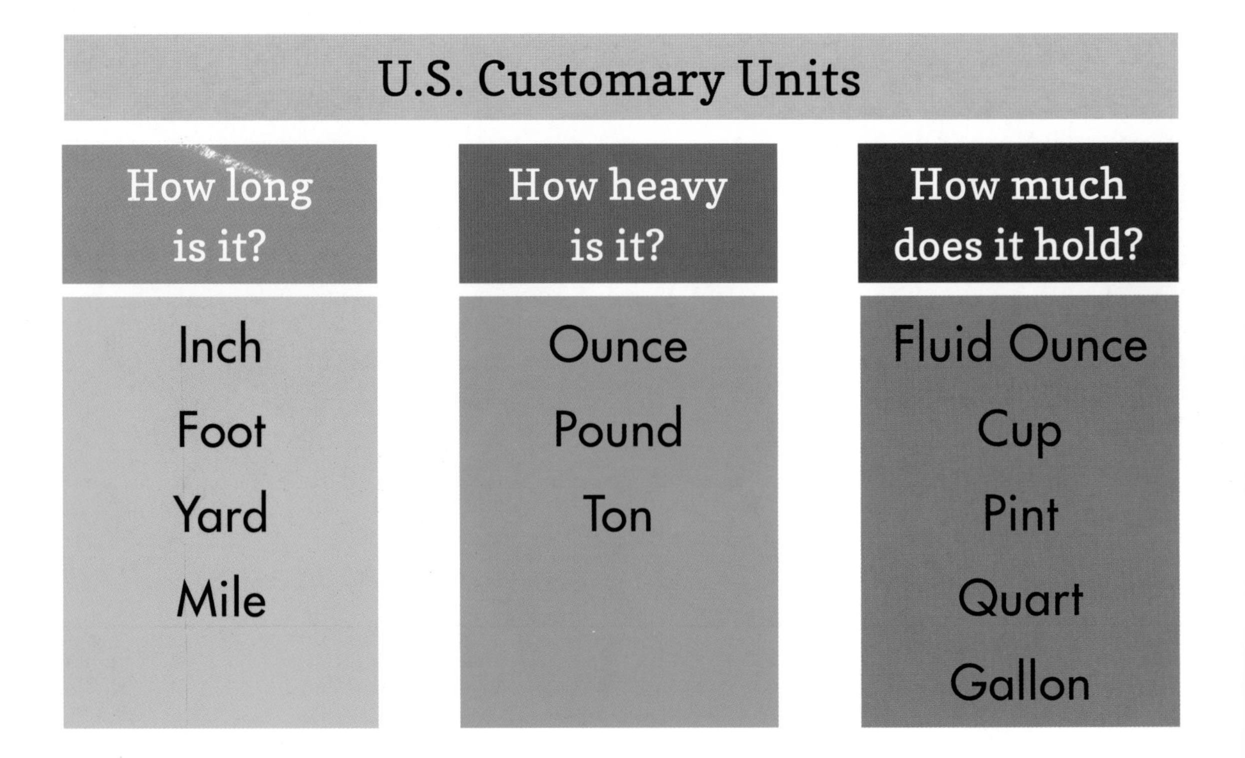

U.S. Customary Units		
How long is it?	How heavy is it?	How much does it hold?
Inch	Ounce	Fluid Ounce
Foot	Pound	Cup
Yard	Ton	Pint
Mile		Quart
		Gallon

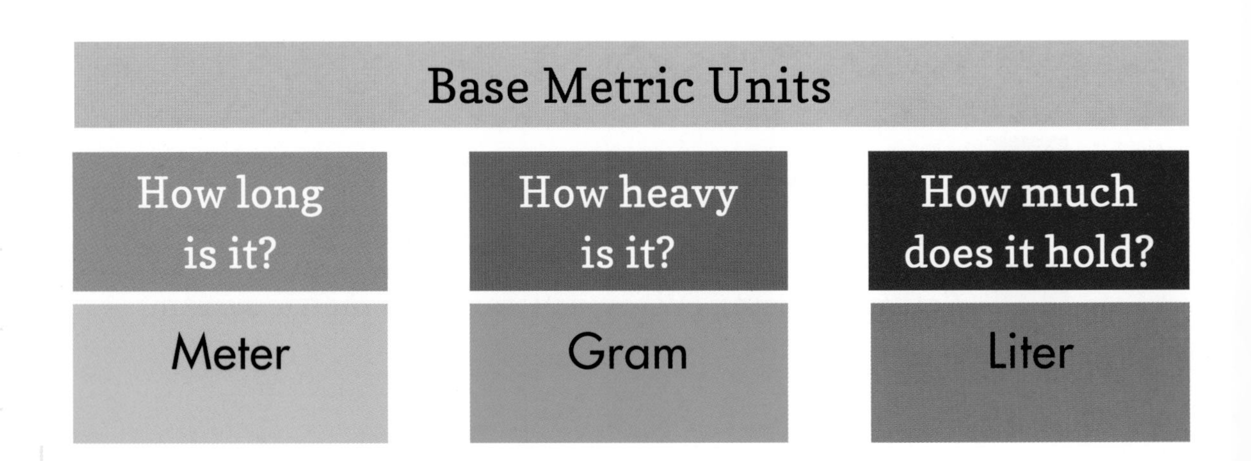

Base Metric Units		
How long is it?	How heavy is it?	How much does it hold?
Meter	Gram	Liter

tickets

Customary Units

Different units you see,
calculate each measurement **precisely**.

Inch, foot, yard, and mile
all measure length of different styles.

The smallest customary measure of length is an inch.
It is used to measure small things in a cinch.

There are 12 inches in a foot,
which measures things a little bigger than a book.

Put three feet together and you have one yard. When measuring in yards, the best trick is to use a yardstick.

Even with a cool yardstick tool, measuring yards is hard to do because yards are used to measure distances less than a mile, from me to you.

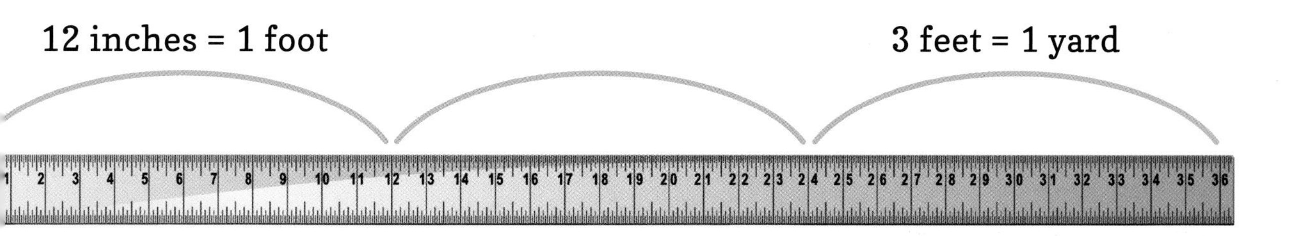

Measuring in miles is the largest measure of length to know. Get in your car and let's get ready to go!

Check It Out!

There are 63,360 inches in one mile. Good thing we can measure in miles because measuring with inches would take a while.

Choose the customary unit you would use to measure each.

Pencil

Feet or Inches?

Scissors

Yards or Inches?

Bottle of Glue

Inches or Miles?

Door

Feet or Miles?

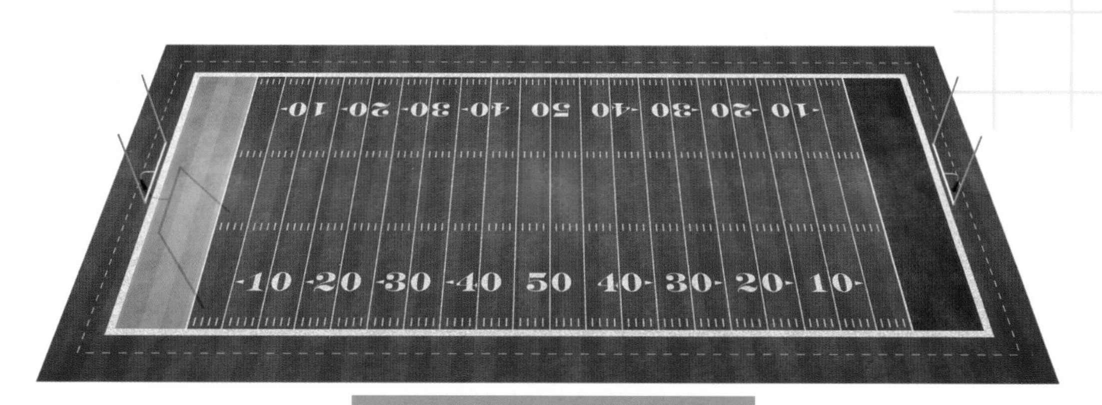

Football Field

Inches or Yards?

Computer Screen

Feet or Inches?

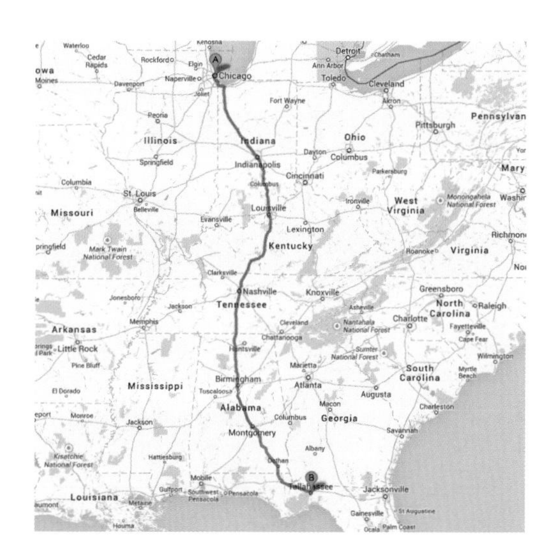

Distance Between Two Cities

Yards or Miles?

Answers:

Inches
Inches
Inches
Feet

Yards
Inches
Miles

Convert Customary Lengths

Customary length is almost done.
Follow these simple steps one by one
for some **conversion** fun!

1. Find the measurement you are starting with on the chart.
2. Multiply to convert to a smaller unit or divide to convert to a larger unit.

Length Conversions
1 foot = 12 inches
1 yard = 36 inches or 3 feet
1 mile = 63,360 inches or 5,280 feet or 1,760 yards

Always Multiply to Convert to Smaller Units			
Feet	to inches multiply by 12		
Yards	to inches multiply by 36	to feet multiply by 3	
Miles	to inches multiply by 63,360	to feet multiply by 5,280	to yards to multiply by 1,760

Always Divide to Convert to Larger Units			
Inches	to feet divide by 12	to yards divide by 36	to miles divide by 63,360
Feet	to yards divide by 3	to miles divide by 5,280	
Yards	to miles divide by 1,760		

We've talked it though, now let's practice a few!

12 yards = ? feet

Multiply to convert to smaller units.

$12 \times 3 = 36$

12 yards = 36 feet

240 inches = ? feet

Divide to convert to smaller units.

$240 \div 12 = 20$

240 inches = 20 feet

Pick the correction conversion.

Length Conversions
1 foot = 12 inches
1 yard = 36 inches or 3 feet
1 mile = 63,360 inches or 5,280 feet or 1,760 yards

25 yards = ? feet

3 or 75?

144 inches = ? feet

12 or 432?

6 feet = ? inches

2 or 72?

2 miles = ? feet
10,560 or 2,640?

4 yards = ? inches
9 or 144?

9 feet = ? yards
3 or 27?

Answers:
75 feet
12 feet
72 inches
10,560 feet
144 inches
3 yards

Customary Weight

The debate goes on that **mass** is not weight,
but as long as you are on Earth either will equate.

Get ready to hop on a scale
to find out about customary weight in detail.

Ounce, pound, and ton is how it is done.

1 strawberry is about 1 ounce

1 loaf of bread is about 1 pound

2 horses are about 1 ton

Convert Customary Weight

The rules are the same. Multiply to go smaller and divide to go bigger.

Weight Conversions
16 ounces = 1 pound
2,000 pounds = 1 ton

Let's talk it through and practice a few!

2 pounds = ? ounces

Ounces are smaller than pounds, so you will need to multiply. Check the chart. Since 16 ounces is equal to a pound, multiply pounds by 16.

2 × 16 = 32

2 pounds = 32 ounces

4,000 pounds = ? tons

Tons are larger than pounds, so you will need to divide. Check the chart. Since 2,000 pounds is equal to a ton, divide tons by 2,000.

4,000 ÷ 2,000 = 2

4,000 pounds = 2 tons

---

160 ounces = ? pounds

Pounds are larger than ounces, so you will need to divide. Check the chart. Since 16 ounces equal a pound, divide pounds by 16.

160 ÷ 16 = 10

160 ounces = 10 pounds

Customary Capacity

Capacity is controlled
by how much a container can really hold.

Customary capacity is measured in fluid ounces, cups, pints, quarts, and gallons.

1 cup
8 ounces

1 pint
2 cups
16 ounces

1 quart
2 pints
4 cups
32 ounces

1 gallon
4 quarts
8 pints
16 cups
128 ounces

Convert Customary Capacity

With the help of this picture, count the letters you see to convert most every measure of capacity.

G = gallon **Q = quarts** **P = pints** **C = cups**

Count the letters found inside each measure and you will soon agree:

2 cups equal 1 pint
2 pints equal 1 quart
4 cups equal 1 quart
4 quarts equal 1 gallon
8 pints equal 1 gallon
16 cups equal 1 gallon

Metric Units

Now we will see just how the world calculates measurement differently.

It is such a pleasure to have just one base unit for each type of measure.

Length	Weight	Capacity
Meter	Gram	Liter

The size of each unit is based on 10.
For each size larger you go, grab a pen and divide by 10.

For each size smaller you go, grab a pen and multiply by 10.

Let's take a moment to show
how a **meter**, **gram**, or **liter** can grow.

The order of the sizes will never change.

Meter	Gram	Liter
Kilometer 25	**Kilogram** 25	**Kiloliter** 25
Hectameter 250	**Hectagram** 250	**Hectaliter** 250
Dekameter 2,500	**Dekagram** 2,500	**Dekaliter** 2,500
Meter 25,000	**Gram** 25,000	**Liter** 25,000
Decimeter 250,000	**Decigram** 250,000	**Deciliter** 250,000
Centimeter 2,500,000	**Centigram** 2,500,000	**Centiliter** 2,500,000
Millimeter 25,000,000	**Milligram** 25,000,000	**Milliliter** 25,000,000

King Henry

Remembering each size can be hard to memorize.

Here is a trick to help remember the chart really quick.

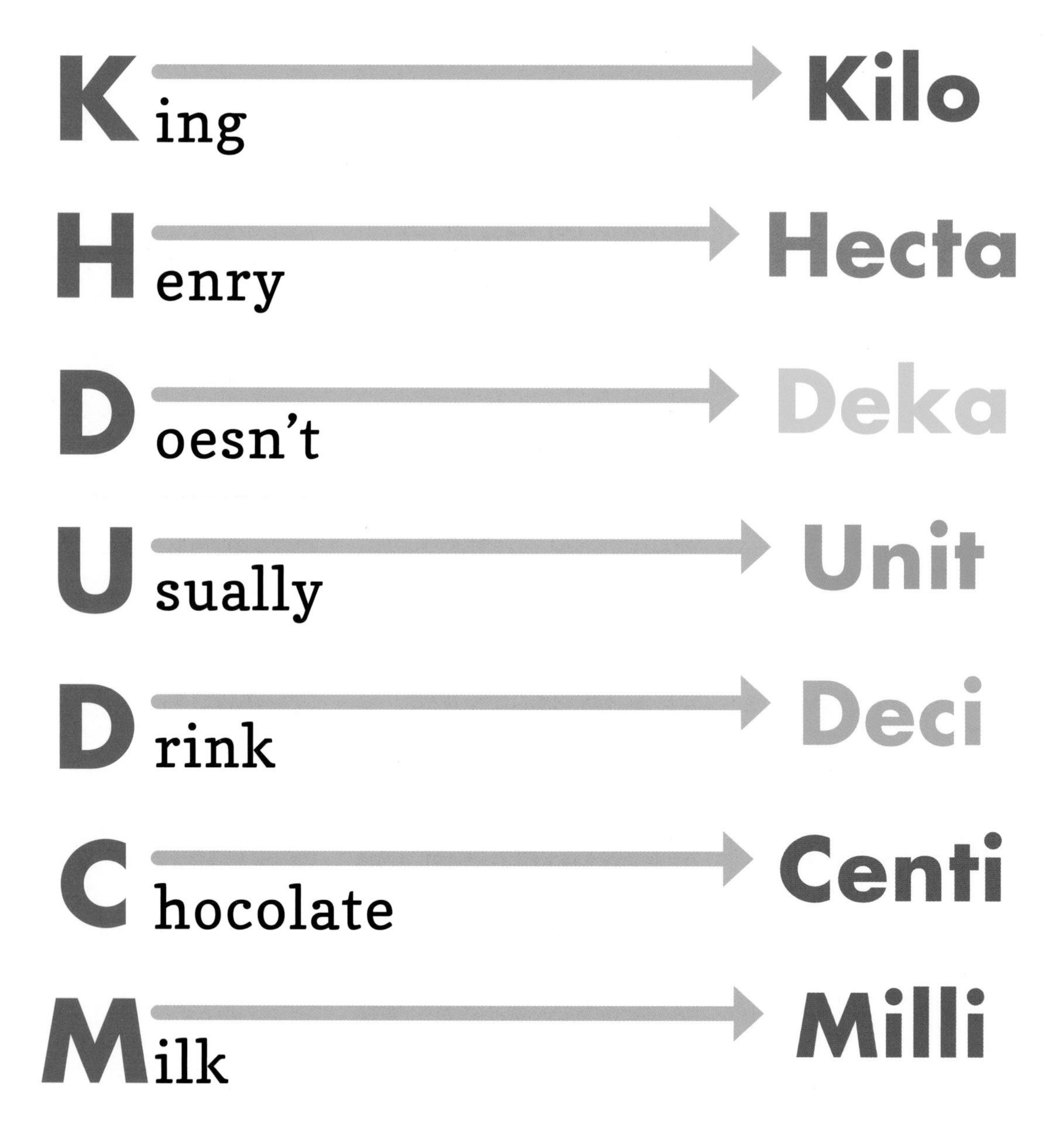

Stair Method

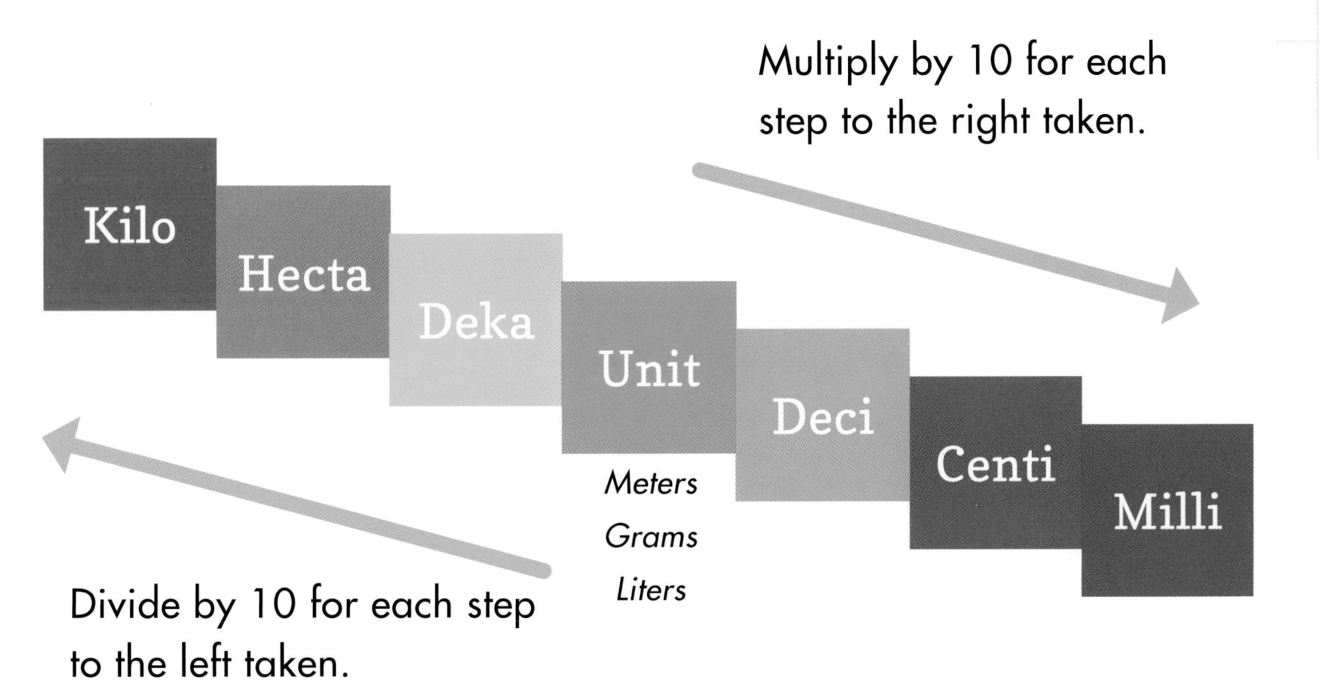

Moving the decimal to the right or left takes care of the math in one quick step.

Convert Metric Units

Here is your chart, so let's get ready to start!

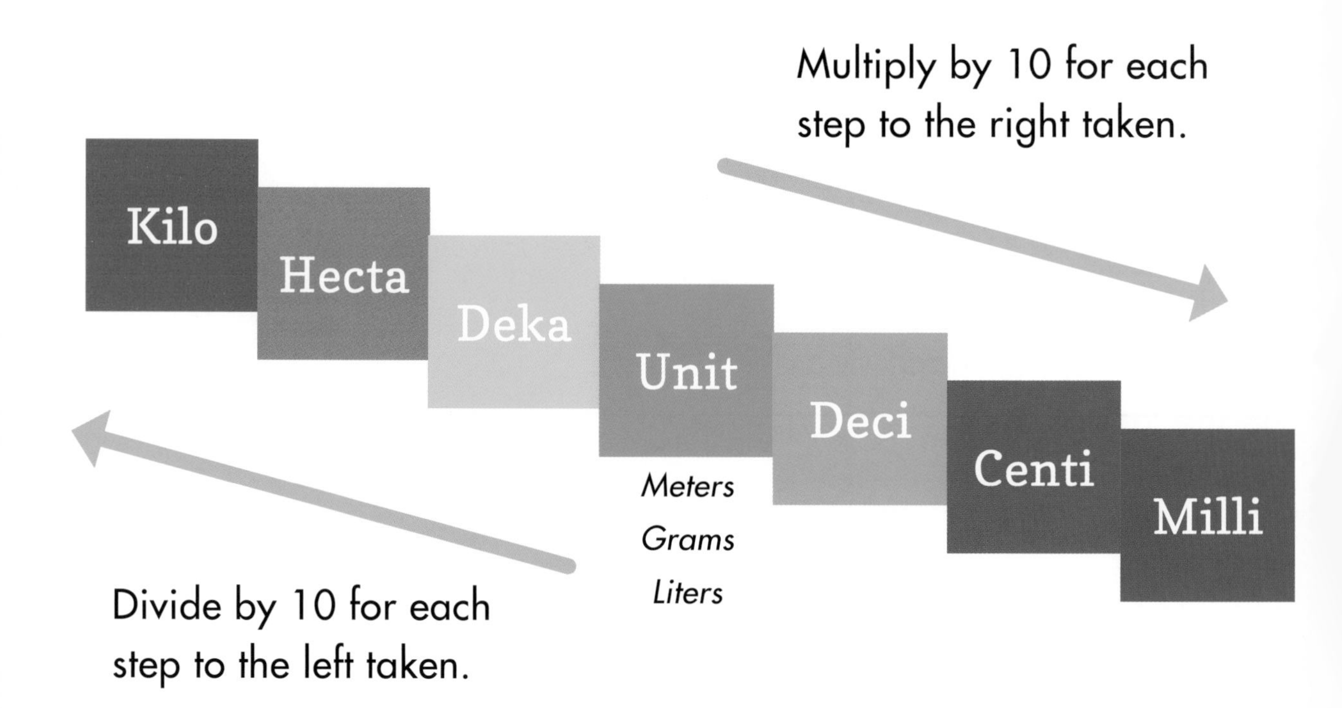

1,000 milligrams = ? grams

100 or 1

1 liter = ? milliliters

1,000 or 100

15 meters = ? centimeters

1,500 or 1.5

25 kilometers = ? meters

2,500 or 25,000

Answers:

1

1,000

1,500

25,000

Glossary

capacity (kuh-PASS-uh-tee): the largest amount that something can hold

conversion (kuhn-VUR-shuhn): to change something into something else

customary units (KUSS-tuh-mer-ee YOO-nits): the measurement system used in the United States

exclusively (ek-SKLOO-siv-lee): entirely

gram (GRAHM): the metric unit used to measure weight

length (lengkth): how long something is

liter (LEE-tur): the metric unit used to measure capacity

mass (MASS): the amount of matter an object has

measurement (MEZH-ur-ment): to measure something

meter (MEE-tur): the metric unit used to measure length

metric system (MET-rik SISS-tuhm): a measurement system based on multiplying and dividing by ten

precisely (pri-SISSE-lee): accurately and exactly

unit (YOO-nit): the standard amount used when measuring

weight (WATE): how heavy an object is

Index

capacity 4, 20, 22, 24
conversion 14, 15, 16, 17, 19
customary units 6, 7, 8, 10
exclusively 6
gram 8, 24
length 4, 10, 11, 14, 24
liter 8, 24, 25, 28
mass 18
measurement 4, 6, 7, 10, 14, 24
meter 8, 24, 29
metric system 6, 7
unit 6, 12, 14, 24
weight 4, 5, 18, 19, 24

Websites to Visit

www.learner.org/interactives/metric/symbols2.html
www.mrnussbaum.com/soup-play
www.mathfox.com/mathgames/metric-system-game

About the Author

Lisa Arias is a math teacher who lives in Tampa, Florida with her husband and two children. Her out-of-the-box thinking and love for math guided her toward becoming an author. She enjoys playing board games and spending time with family and friends.

Meet The Author!
www.meetREMauthors.com

www.rourkeeducationalmedia.com

PHOTO CREDITS: Cover: © lianella, IvonneW, v777999, phillipdyer; Page 4: © bach005, malerapaso; Page 5: © Magdalena Kucova, Narongsak Yaisumlee; Page 9: © Pamela Moore; Page 10: © Alhovik, Maogg; Page 11: © John T Takai, Antagain, GTS; Page 12: © Nichls, Shantell, skodonnell, me4o; Page 13: © ZargonDesign, tiler84; Page 18:© Mariusz Black, Lauri Patterson, GlobalIP; Page 20: © EasyBuy4u, benoitb; Page 12: © Oktay Ortakcioglu, Carlos Alvarez

Edited by: Jill Sherman

Cover and Interior design by: Tara Raymo

Library of Congress PCN Data

Marvelous Measurement: Conversions / Lisa Arias
(Got Math!)
ISBN 978-1-62717-712-2 (hard cover)
ISBN 978-1-62717-834-1 (soft cover)
ISBN 978-1-62717-947-8 (e-Book)
Library of Congress Control Number: 2014935589

Printed in the United States of America, North Mankato, Minnesota

Also Available as: